PRIMARY EXPLORERS

FLAGS
of the World

Authors:
Kirsty Neale and
Brian Williams

Consultant:
Graham Bartram,
The Flag Institute

Some flags kindly supplied
by the Flag Institute.

igloo

CONTENTS

WHAT IS A FLAG?

There are few pieces of fabric that inspire as much feeling as a flag.

For about 5,000 years, people have displayed flags. They can bring nations together, or set them apart during a war, pass on bad news, or be flown in celebration. Flags symbolize history and tradition, and are a way for people around the world to communicate in a common language.

WHAT IS A FLAG?

A flag is a piece of cloth, usually square, rectangular or triangular, and flown from a pole or mast. Its design represents a particular country, group, belief or message and can be influenced by history, geography and religion. The exact shape (or ratio) and design of most national flags is set down in law, along with a set of rules about how the flag should be treated and displayed.

WHY ARE FLAGS FLOWN?

Flags are used for many purposes – as decorations, to send signals, to communicate and to bring together people who share the same goals or interests. National and international flags make it easy to identify a country, a religion, an organization or even a VIP, and flags can also be used to send important messages and warnings, even between people who don't speak the same language.

A flagpole, flagstaff or mast is the metal or wooden pole from which a flag is flown. It may include a pulley to help raise and lower the flag.

The canton is the top left, or upper hoist, corner of the flag. Many marine flags have their national flag in the canton.

The fly is the part of the flag furthest away from the flagpole. It's opposite the hoist, and is sometimes called the fly edge.

The hoist is the side of the flag closest to the flagpole. 'Hoist' can also be used to describe the height of a flag.

A charge is any picture, emblem or figure that appears on the background (also known as the field) of a flag.

A halyard is the rope, or line, used to raise, or hoist, and lower a flag displayed on a flagpole.

During the 16th century, Spain didn't have a national flag, so the king's standard was used instead. The Spanish royal standard was carried to the New World by many Spanish explorers.

The Buddhist flag was designed in 1885 and symbolizes togetherness, love and kindness. It is flown by Buddhists in almost 60 countries around the world. The stripes represent peace (blue), wisdom (orange), balance (yellow), good fortune (red) and freedom (white).

WHO USES FLAGS?

Flags are flown all over the world by all kinds of people – schoolchildren, shopkeepers, soldiers, sports stars, presidents and royalty. They are waved by crowds to show support for a national hero or team, and displayed outside government buildings to welcome VIPs from other countries. Royal flags are flown over a palace to mark whether the king or queen is in residence and, at sea, all ships must fly a flag to identify their nationality. When a country is in mourning, flags are flown at half-mast.

Prayer flags are made and flown by Buddhists in the Himalayas. They are believed to spread peace, kindness and wisdom as they flutter in the wind.

Cars used by kings, queens and emperors often fly a small version of the royal or imperial flag so they can be easily identified.

WHERE TO LOOK FOR FLAGS

Once you start looking for flags, you'll see them all over the place. They fly in parks and squares, outside important buildings, on cars, boats and ships. They're used to send signals on racetracks, beaches and snowy mountains. People wave flags at sporting events, festivals, parades, processions and to celebrate national holidays. They're used on shrines, in churches and for serious occasions, such as funerals. Some countries use their national flag design on car number plates, or as a mark to show where goods were made.

The Japanese imperial flag has been used by the emperor and his family for over 100 years.

DESIGNS AND SHAPES

Every flag contains 'coded' information in its shape and design.

The shapes and symbols on flags have special names and meanings. Many national flags use traditional patterns or designs, which can give clues to their history. Familiar patterns include the Greek cross, the Scandinavian cross, three vertical bands, three horizontal bands, and quarters. The US flag, or 'Stars and Stripes,' has a canton (the blue rectangle with white stars) and a background or field of red and white stripes.

Serration This flag has a zigzag (saw-tooth) design, with two bands.

HOISTING A FLAG

A flag is raised (hoisted) briskly, and lowered slowly. It should be gathered and folded before it touches the ground. Flying a flag at 'half-mast' is a sign of mourning for the death of a person.

Triangle On this flag, diagonal lines from two corners make three triangles.

Couped cross In this design, the cross arms stop short of the flag edges.

Double-banded Two bands, either vertical or horizontal, as here.

Quartered A flag design with four equal parts.

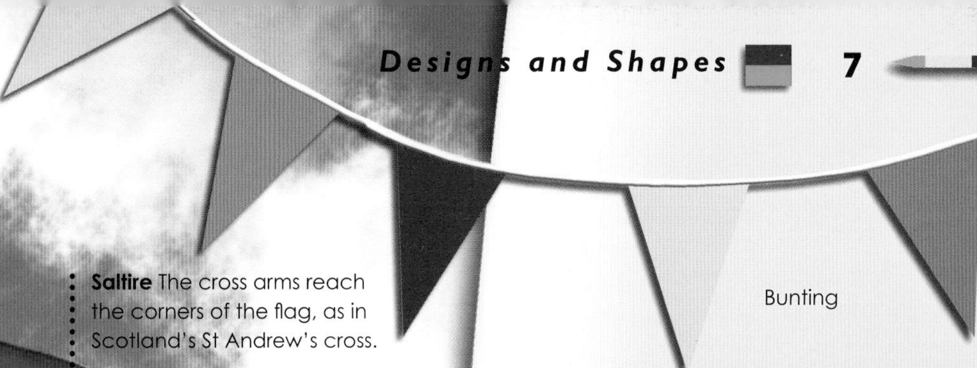

Horizontal tri-band Three bands arranged horizontally.

Saltire The cross arms reach the corners of the flag, as in Scotland's St Andrew's cross.

Bunting

FLAG SHAPES
Most modern flags are rectangular. Other shapes include the medieval gonfalon, which hangs down, the square banner (a warrior's battle-flag), and the burgee, often flown on sailing boats.

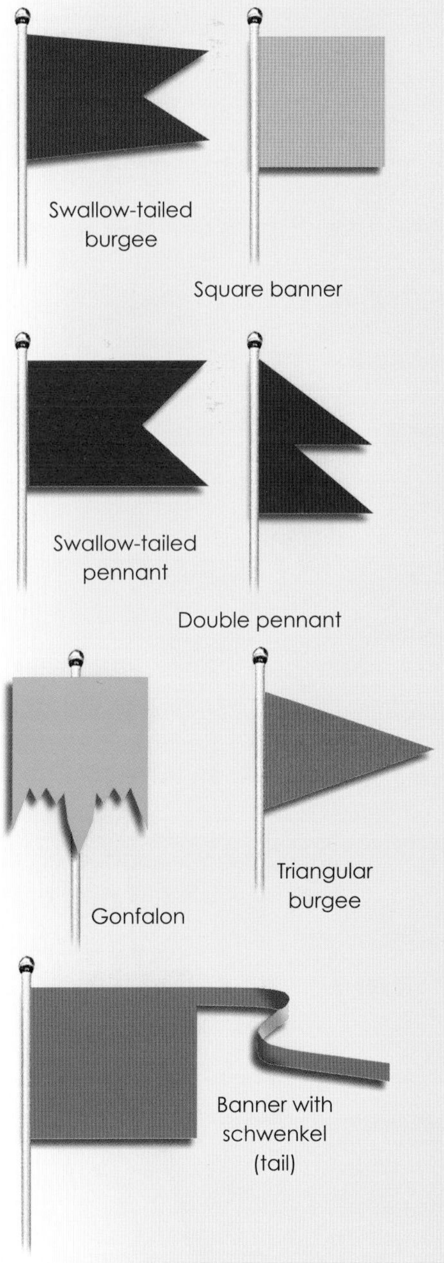

Vertical tricolore (or tri-band) Three bands arranged vertically.

Fimbriated A narrow line (white here) separates one element from another.

Swallow-tailed burgee

Square banner

Swallow-tailed pennant

Double pennant

Bordered The flag has a distinct border around its four edges.

Gonfalon

Triangular burgee

Scandinavian cross The cross has arms of unequal length, reaching the flag edges.

Banner with schwenkel (tail)

FLAGS IN HISTORY

In history, some flags have inspired bravery. Others have made people quake with fear.

Flags were carried by soldiers into battle, helping them to identify friends and enemies as armies clashed. Flags were also waved to send signals, paraded to celebrate a victory, and flown by rulers as a show of strength to the world. Over time, they became national emblems.

FIRST CLOTH FLAGS

As well as their eagle standards (called *aquila*), the Romans also had the first cloth flags, which hung from a cross-bar. The Roman word for them was *vexilla*, and from this come the words 'vexillology', which means the study of flags, and 'vexilloid', a long pole topped by a carving.

A Roman standard-bearer carries a *vexillum* flag to identify the legion. Standard-bearers wore the hide of an animal, such as a bear or lion.

On this ancient Greek coin, a soldier is seen carrying a pole with a flaglike device attached.

The world's oldest flag is from Persia (modern Iran). It is made of metal, and has survived for 5,000 years.

EARLY FLAGS

Some of the earliest-known 'flags' belonged to the Egyptian pharaohs about 5,000 years ago. Their flag-bearers carried long poles topped by carvings, often of a god. A thousand years later, decorated poles, or standards, were carried by Roman legions (army units of about 5,000 men) as they conquered and defended their mighty empire.

Roman legions carried a standard topped by an eagle. It was a terrible disgrace for a legion to lose its standard to the enemy.

PIRATE FLAGS

The skull and crossbones

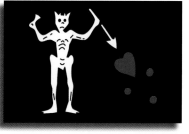

Blackbeard's flag

Pirates roaming the seas hoisted scary flags, such as the skull and crossbones, to frighten the enemy into surrendering. French pirates flew a blood-red flag called the '*joulie rouge*', which became known in English as the 'jolly roger'. Famous pirates, such as Blackbeard (Edward Teach), designed their own flags.

A Japanese samurai warrior fought with a battle flag on his back to show who he was.

Two of the US Civil War battle flags were the Confederate (Southern) battle flag (left), and the Union (Northern) flag or 'Stars and Stripes' (right).

Samurai flags included long banners. Generals usually had square flags. Flags helped a general to see where his soldiers were on the battlefield.

Warlords in Japan (900s–1800s) were called daimyos. Each warrior in a daimyo family had a personal flag, with symbols called mon.

At Gettysburg (July 1863), Confederate troops carried their flag into battle. The Union army won. It was a turning point in the Civil War.

CIVIL WAR FLAGS

When the American Civil War began in 1861, the Confederate (Southern) states adopted their own flag as a sign of their break with the states of the Union. The first Confederate flag, called the 'Stars and Bars', looked too much like the Union flag and caused confusion in battle, so the Confederates adopted a new red battle flag with a blue cross and 13 stars. Each star represented one of the breakaway Southern states.

HERALDIC FLAGS

Heraldic emblems and flags helped identify medieval knights. The language of heraldry is all about symbols.

In battle, knights clad in metal could not easily tell friend from foe. So each knight took to wearing special emblems, like badges, to show who they were. The emblems were sewn onto cloth and painted onto shields. Away from the battlefield, the emblems became family heraldic symbols.

KNIGHTS AND THEIR BANNERS

Banners were flags carried into battle – the bigger the banner, the more important its owner. A lowly knight's flag had small swallow-tails, and was called a pennon. If the knight showed great courage in battle, his king might cut off the tails, turning the pennon into a banner. He was then a 'Knight Banneret', and could command a troop of other fighting men. In medieval Europe, some knights formed religious orders, such as the Knights Templars. They fought in the wars known as the Crusades.

SYMBOLS

Label (oldest son)	Crescent (2nd son)	Mullet (3rd son)
Martlet (4th son)	Annulet (5th son)	Fleur-de-lis (6th son)

Some of the symbols on a coat of arms were signs of rank or status. They were called cadency symbols, and different symbols could be added to brothers' coats of arms to show each brother's rank in the family.

COATS OF ARMS

A knight wore a cloth surcoat ('top coat') with a personal emblem. These came to be known as coats of arms. Each is a unique design made up of heraldic devices.

Chief The top part of a shield, often signifying authority.

Supporters Animals or humans that hold up a shield – here, a lion and a unicorn.

Crest The topmost element, often a crown or other symbol of power, such as a lion.

Shield Also known as the escutcheon, the main part of any coat of arms.

Scroll A curling band with a motto, often written in Latin.

A knight's banner bore a personal emblem, sometimes with a religious symbol as well.

Crusaders carried the Christian cross. By the 1500s, heraldic devices were less often worn in battle.

A surcoat was a cloth garment worn by a knight. His horse wore the same heraldic devices on its coat.

SHAPES AND EMBLEMS

The shape of a heraldic flag could be as important as its emblems. The most important flag was the king's royal standard.

Standard

A standard was a very large, tapering flag. It was fixed into the ground before battle, to show where the king was on the battlefield.

Banner

Banners, square or oblong, were carried into battle – unlike standards, which were too big. This banner bears the royal fleur-de-lis (lily) of France.

Oriflamme

The French oriflamme ('golden flame') battle flag was long with trailing points ending in tassels. First used in 1124, its message was 'no prisoners.'

NORTH AMERICA

North America's two biggest nations have flags that reflect their history.

The popular name for the United States' flag is the 'Stars and Stripes'. Other names are the 'Star-Spangled Banner' and 'Old Glory'. The first official US flag was made in 1777, since when it has changed many times (see opposite). Canada has seen a number of flag changes, too. From 1534 until the early 1760s, when the French governed the region, the fleur-de-lis was flown. When the British took control, they flew the Royal Union flag, or Union Jack. The maple leaf flag was adopted in 1965.

1 Canada
2 United States of America

Canada is the world's 2nd largest country. The USA is the 4th biggest.

CANADA'S FLAG

The Canadian Red Ensign

From 1868 to 1965, the Canadian Red Ensign was widely flown in Canada, although until 1946 the official flag was the Royal Union flag, or Union Jack. In 1964, the government chose the maple leaf flag.

Maple leaf flags are everywhere as Canadians celebrate Canada Day (July 1).

Canada's maple leaf flag

Americans fly the flag on many occasions, especially at election rallies, such as this for President Obama.

PLEDGING ALLEGIANCE TO THE FLAG

The US has a flag code, a set of rules about when and how the national flag should be flown. For example, there are rules about flying flags at half-mast, parading the flag, saluting the flag, and the use of the flag at funerals. American schoolchildren have recited the Pledge of Allegiance to the flag since 1892. The pledge is a solemn promise of loyalty to the United States. As they make the pledge, the children stand to attention facing the flag and hold their right hand over their heart. People in uniform salute the flag as a sign of respect.

People wave the flag to express patriotism – the pride and love they feel for their country.

STARS AND STRIPES

The 'Stars and Stripes' flag has been altered many times in its history, as the United States grew from 13 ex-colonies to a Union of 50 states.

Grand Union flag

The Grand Union flag was used when war with Britain began in 1775.

'Betsy Ross' flag

Supposedly a flagmaker named Betsy Ross sewed on the stars, in 1776.

13 stars flag

The 13 stars and stripes of the 1777 flag stood for the 13 colonies that fought for independence from Britain.

15 stars flag

The 1795 flag had 15 stars and stripes, for the then 15 states.

50 stars, 50 states

In 1960, after Hawaii became the 50th state, the flag had 50 stars.

US STATE FLAGS

Each of the 50 states of the United States has its own historic flag.

States, provinces and many cities have flags that tell something of their history. Many of the US state flags include the state's seal, or badge. Some have a number of stars to show in what order they joined the Union. New Hampshire, for example, has nine stars to show it was the 9th state to join. The year that each state adopted its flag is included in the flag descriptions, below and opposite.

MOUNT RUSHMORE

All the US state flags are displayed at the Mount Rushmore National Memorial, a huge granite monument to four US presidents in South Dakota.

1 Alaska

The state flag of Alaska (1927) shows the Big Dipper, or Great Bear, and the North Star.

2 Washington

Washington's state flag (1923) features green for forests and the head of George Washington.

3 Oregon

The Oregon state flag (1925) shows the state seal and the date of statehood, 1859. On the reverse is a beaver.

4 California

The state flag of California (1911) includes its 1846 name, when it broke from Spain.

5 Idaho

The Idaho state flag (1907) shows the state seal, which includes a miner and a woman representing justice.

6 Nevada

The Nevada state flag (1929) shows a silver star and the words 'Battle Born' above it.

7 Montana

The Montana state flag (1905) shows the state seal with the state's name, added in 1981.

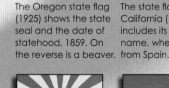  

8 Wyoming

Wyoming's state flag (1917) shows a buffalo (bison). Vast herds once roamed the prairies.

9 Utah

The state flag of Utah (1913) bears the state seal, which includes a bald eagle, lilies and a beehive.

10 Arizona

On Arizona's state flag (1917), the red and yellow setting sun represents Spain's past in Arizona.

11 Colorado

On the Colorado state flag (1911), the red C stands for Colorado, the yellow for gold.

12 New Mexico

The state flag of New Mexico (1925) shows a Pueblo symbol, and uses crimson and gold (for Spain).

13 North Dakota

The state flag of North Dakota (1911) has a modified version of the US coat of arms. It includes a bald eagle.

14 South Dakota

On the sky blue state flag of South Dakota (1992), the Sun's golden rays surround the state seal.

15 Nebraska

The state flag of Nebraska (1925) bears the state seal showing a smith with a hammer and pioneer life.

16 Kansas

On the Kansas state flag (1927), the rising Sun represents the East, the starting point for most settlers.

17 Oklahoma

The state flag of Oklahoma (1925) bears an Osage warrior's shield and symbols of peace.

18 Texas

The state flag of Texas (1839) is known as the 'Lone Star' flag (Texas is the 'Lone Star State').

19 Minnesota

The Minnesota state flag (1957) has the state seal and dates, including date of statehood (1858).

20 Iowa

On the state flag of Iowa (1921), the eagle and streamer were taken from the state seal.

21 Missouri

On the state flag of Missouri (1913), the 24 stars show it was the 24th state to join the Union.

22 Arkansas

On the Arkansas state flag (1913), the diamond shape represents the state's mining industry.

23 Louisiana

The Louisiana state flag (1912) shows a pelican, and the motto 'Union, Justice & Confidence.'

24 Michigan

On the seal of the Michigan state flag (1911) is a Latin motto meaning 'I Will Defend.'

25 Wisconsin

On Wisconsin's state flag (1913), the name and date of statehood were added in 1981.

26 Illinois

The Illinois state flag (1915) has the state seal with a bald eagle. 'Illinois' was added in 1970.

27 Indiana

The Indiana state flag (1917) has a torch of freedom and 19 stars. Indiana was the 19th state to join the Union.

28 Kentucky

On the state flag of Kentucky (1918), the state seal shows a frontiersman and a statesman.

Fifty states make up the United States. Separate in geography are Alaska in the northwest and the island state of Hawaii in the Pacific Ocean.

1 Alaska
2 Washington
3 Oregon
4 California
5 Idaho
6 Nevada
7 Montana
8 Wyoming
9 Utah
10 Arizona
11 Colorado
12 New Mexico
13 North Dakota
14 South Dakota
15 Nebraska
16 Kansas
17 Oklahoma
18 Texas
19 Minnesota
20 Iowa
21 Missouri
22 Arkansas
23 Louisiana
24 Michigan
25 Wisconsin
26 Illinois
27 Indiana
28 Kentucky
29 Tennessee
30 Mississippi
31 Alabama
32 Ohio
33 West Virginia
34 Virginia
35 North Carolina
36 South Carolina
37 Georgia
38 Florida
39 Tennessee
40 Mississippi
41 Vermont
42 Maine
43 New Hampshire
44 Massachusetts
45 Rhode Island
46 Connecticut
47 New Jersey
48 Delaware
49 Maryland
50 Hawaii

Washington DC

29 Tennessee

On the Tennessee state flag (1905), the stars represent East, Middle and West Tennessee.

30 Mississippi

The state flag of Mississippi (1894) has a Confederate flag with 13 stars in the upper left portion.

31 Alabama

The Alabama state flag (1895) has a red cross echoing the Confederates' Civil War battle flag.

32 Ohio

Ohio's state flag (1902) shows 17 stars (for the 17th state). It is the only state flag of this shape.

33 West Virginia

The seal on West Virginia's state flag (1929) includes images of a miner and a farmer.

34 Virginia

On Virginia's state flag (1931), the seal shows Virtue triumphant over Tyranny.

35 North Carolina

On North Carolina's state flag (1885), the dates refer to events in the War of Independence.

(Enlarged view)

50 Hawaii

The state flag of Hawaii (1959) shows a British flag, representing Captain Cook (1778 discoverer), and stripes for the 8 main islands.

36 South Carolina

South Carolina's blue state flag (1861) shows a white palmetto tree and a crescent moon.

37 Georgia

The Georgia state flag (2003) shows the state coat of arms, which includes 13 stars on the seal.

38 Florida

On the Florida state flag (1899), the state seal (changed in 1985) shows a Native American.

39 Pennsylvania

The Pennsylvania state flag (1907) shows the state seal supported by horses, and an eagle.

40 New York

On the state flag of New York (1909), the figures on the coat of arms are Liberty and Justice.

41 Vermont

Vermont's state flag (1923) has the state coat of arms with a pine tree, wheat sheaves and a cow.

42 Maine

The state flag of Maine (1909) shows a seaman and a farmer, a pine tree and a moose.

43 New Hampshire

On the New Hampshire state flag (1909), the laurel wreath has 9 stars, for the 9th state.

44 Massachusetts

On the Massachusetts state flag (1971), the shield shows a Native American with bow and arrow, and a star.

45 Rhode Island

The state flag of Rhode Island (1897) shows 13 stars for the original 13 colonies, and an anchor.

46 Connecticut

On the state flag of Connecticut (1897), the grapevines symbolize European colonization.

47 New Jersey

On the state flag of New Jersey (1896), the seal shows Liberty and Ceres, goddess of agriculture.

48 Delaware

Delaware's state flag (1913) shows a soldier and a farmer. Delaware was the first state of the Union.

49 Maryland

The Maryland state flag (1904) shows the coats of arms of the Calvert and Crossland families.

MEXICO AND CENTRAL AMERICA

From 1823 to 1840, the countries of Nicaragua, Guatemala, Honduras, El Salvador and Costa Rica joined together to form The United Provinces of Central America. Their blue and white flag represented a land between two seas, and each of the five countries still uses a similar design.

The countries of Central America fought hard to establish their independence and are proud to fly flags with emblems inspired by their history.

Honduras

The flag of Honduras is the oldest in Central America. The five stars represent the United Provinces.

THE FIGHT FOR FREEDOM

Spain was the ruling power in Mexico and Central America for over 300 years, but in 1810, the Mexicans began a war to win their independence. As they battled, the standard of their leader, Miguel Hidalgo, became the symbol of the Mexican army and the country they were fighting for. When the war was finally won, each Central American country adopted its own flag, adding symbols that were important to their nation and its traditions.

The eagle, snake and cactus emblem on the Mexican flag is the Aztec symbol for Mexico City.

Mexico

The flag of Mexico looks similar to the Italian flag, but the red and green stripes are darker and the flag is more rectangular in shape.

Costa Rica

The Costa Rican flag was inspired by the red, white and blue French *tricolore*. The stripes represent hard work (blue), peace (white) and generosity (red).

Honduras celebrates Independence Day on 15th September. Flags are waved at parades all around the country.

9 Bahamas
10 Cuba
11 Jamaica
12 Haiti
13 Dominican Republic
14 St Kitts and Nevis
15 Antigua and Barbuda
16 Dominica
17 St Lucia
18 Barbados
19 St Vincent and the Grenadines
20 Grenada
21 Trinidad and Tobago

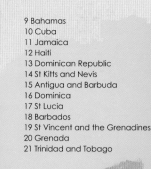

1 Mexico
2 Guatemala
3 Belize
4 Honduras
5 El Salvador
6 Nicaragua
7 Costa Rica
8 Panama

THE CARIBBEAN ISLANDS

The Caribbean lies to the east of Central America and is made up of over 7,000 islands. Some of them are dependent territories, which means they're ruled by another country, and this often reflects in their flag. For instance, the flag of the British-ruled Cayman Islands features a Union Jack and the Cayman coat of arms.

CARIBBEAN FLAGS

Most of the islands in the Caribbean belong to one of 13 independent nations, each of which has its own flag.

Bahamas   Haiti

Trinidad and   Jamaica
Tobago

Nicaragua

The Nicaraguan flag features five volcanoes. The rainbow and sunrays stand for peace and a bright future.

Belize

The flag of Belize is the only national flag to depict human beings. It features loggers, tools and a mahogany tree.

Nicaragua is famous for its 25 volcanoes, which is why they feature on the national flag. Concepcion (above), the country's second-largest volcano, sits on Ometepe island in the middle of Lake Nicaragua.

Guatemala

The coat of arms on the Guatemalan flag shows the date of Central American independence (September 15, 1821).

The resplendent quetzal is the national bird of Guatemala. It features on the national flag. The country's currency, the Guatemalan quetzal, is named after the bird.

SOUTH AMERICA

The flags of South America reflect its lively spirit.

South America has an amazing history, from the ancient Aztec and Inca civilizations, to fighting for independence during the 1800s. Many of its flags reflect this. Colombia, Venezuela and Ecuador have similar red, yellow and blue flags. All three countries once belonged to a nation called Gran Colombia. It only lasted twelve years, but the three versions of its flag have survived for almost two hundred years.

The Sun of May is one of Argentina's national emblems. It symbolizes the Inca Sun-god, Inti, and appears in the middle of the Argentine flag. The flag flies next to a statue of General Belgrano in the Argentine capital, Buenos Aires.

CHILE'S LONE STAR

The flag of Chile was first flown in 1817. It is known as 'the Lone Star', and is similar to the flag of the US state of Texas (see page 14), which has the same name. Chileans are required by law to display their flag on Independence Day (September 18).

Chilean national flag

PASSIONATE BRAZILIANS

The bold and striking Brazilian flag was first hoisted in 1889. The motto '*Ordem e Progresso*' means 'Order and Progress', and the 27 stars represent Brazil's capital and 26 states. Brazilians fly their flag passionately at football matches and national celebrations, such as Independence Day.

Forest covers more than a quarter of Brazil, and is represented by the flag's green background. The yellow stands for wealth and blue is for the sky overhead.

ARGENTINE HERO CREATES NEW FLAG

The Argentinean flag was designed by General Manuel Belgrano. He led the country during the Argentine War of Independence, from 1810 to 1818. During one battle, he realized that his troops were fighting under a red-and-yellow flag, just like the Spanish rulers they were battling against. To avoid confusion, he created a new flag, which was first hoisted near Rosario in 1812. After the war was won, General Belgrano's design was adopted as the national flag. His bands of blue and white have been flown in Argentina ever since.

WIPHALA FLAGS

A wiphala is a square flag traditionally used by the native peoples of the Andes and Amazon regions of South America. It can either be made up of seven horizontal stripes in rainbow shades, or a rainbow grid pattern, seven small squares wide by seven small squares tall. Some people believe it dates back hundreds of years to the time of the Inca civilization.

The Bolivian wiphala is often flown alongside Bolivia's red, yellow and green state flag.

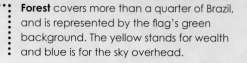

SOUTH AMERICA
The countries of South America are joined in the Union of South American Nations.

1 Colombia
2 Venezuela
3 Guyana
4 Suriname
5 French Guiana *
6 Ecuador
7 Peru
8 Brazil

9 Bolivia
10 Paraguay
11 Chile
12 Argentina
13 Uruguay

* French Guiana is an overseas department of France.

Venezuela

The red stands for independence, yellow for wealth and blue for courage.

Peru

Peru celebrates National Flag Day on June 7 each year.

Bolivia

The Bolivian national flag was first flown in 1851.

NORTHERN AFRICA

Of Africa's 53 countries, more than half are in the north of the region.

Many of the African nations were once ruled by European countries, such as France and the United Kingdom, and others have close connections with the Arab world. You can see signs of this both in their languages and in their flags.

EUROPEAN AND ARAB INFLUENCES

In the French-speaking countries of Chad and Mali, the national flags are inspired by France's *tricolore* – they both have three vertical bands of equal width. The flag of Senegal is the same as Mali's, except for the addition of a green star in the central band, representing Islam. The Arab influence is probably strongest in the north of the region. In Libya, for example, the national flag is plain green, reflecting the people's devotion to Islam.

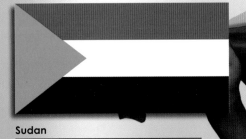

Sudan

Sudan's red, white black and green flag was adopted in 1970. Sudan has close links with Egypt, and the two countries have similar flags.

A UNIVERSAL SYMBOL

In August 1920, a society called UNIA (the Universal Negro Improvement Association) created a new banner for a special meeting they were holding. The society was fighting for equal rights and support among the people of Africa, and the flag quickly became the official flag of the African race. It was made up of three horizontal bands of red, black and green, and today is known as the Pan-African, Universal African or International African flag.

THE AFRICAN-AMERICAN FLAG

The Pan-African flag is flown and recognized all over the world by people of African descent. In 2000, an artist named David Hammons created a special version of the American flag with African-inspired stars and stripes in red, black and green.

1 Western Sahara *
2 Morocco
3 Algeria
4 Tunisia
5 Libya
6 Egypt

7 Mauritania
8 Mali
9 Burkina Faso
10 Niger
11 Chad
12 Sudan
13 Eritrea
14 Djibouti
15 Ethiopia
16 Somalia
17 Senegal
18 Cape Verde
19 Gambia

20 Guinea Bissau
21 Guinea
22 Sierra Leone
23 Liberia
24 Côte d'Ivoire
25 Ghana
26 Togo
27 Benin
28 Nigeria
29 Cameroon
30 Central African Republic

* Western Sahara is a
disputed territory.

Northern Africa has some very large countries. Sudan, the biggest, is also the largest country in Africa and the largest in the Arab World.

When Sudanese athlete Abubaker Kaki Khamis set a world record in 2008, he proudly displayed Sudan's national flag. The crowd showed its support by waving flags, too.

North African flags
Some of the region's flags are shown below.

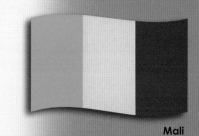

Mali
Mali's flag used to feature a black *kanaga*, or stick figure, in the middle.

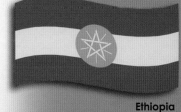

Ethiopia
The blue and yellow emblem stands for peace, togetherness and success.

Egypt
Egypt's flag features the national coat of arms, the golden eagle of Saladin.

Algeria
The red star and crescent represent Islam, Algeria's national religion.

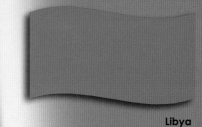

Libya
Libya is the only country in the world to fly a completely plain flag.

PAN AFRICA

The flags of many African countries use green, red and yellow, from the flag of Ethiopia. Green stands for the crops grown by the farmers. Red stands for blood shed as people fought to win their freedom. Yellow symbolizes riches and the sun's warmth.

Countries shown in orange feature red, yellow, and green in their national flags. Some of them also feature black.

Benin
The national flag of Benin has a bold, simple design and uses Pan-African red, yellow and green.

SOUTHERN AFRICA

Southern Africa is a region of huge contrasts, many of which are reflected in its flags.

There are many native peoples in southern Africa, such as the Zulu and Bantu people, as well as European and Asian settlers. Their traditions and history, and the land itself, have all influenced the national flags. Lush vegetation and the oceans are often represented by green and blue, as on the flags of Mauritius and Namibia. Gold is sometimes used to represent mineral wealth.

Air Namibia flies the flag on every trip! As the country's national airline, it has a version of the flag painted on the tail of all its planes.

Botswana

Most of Botswana is covered in desert. Water is a very precious resource, and this is represented by blue on the national flag.

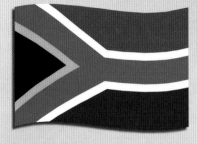

South Africa

By law, South Africa's national flag must be treated with dignity and respect. Official permission is needed to use the flag's design.

Madagascar

The red and white bands represent the ancient kings and queens of Madagascar. The green band stands for the hard-working people.

Black and white on Botswana's flag stand for racial harmony, and also refer to zebras, which support Botswana's coat of arms.

A FLAG FOR FREEDOM

South African Freedom Day is celebrated every year on April 27. It commemorates the government election held on that date in 1994, when black and white people had equal rights to vote for the first time. To mark this important change in the history of South Africa, a competition was held to design a new national flag. More than 7,000 people entered. The winning design quickly became a symbol of the new South Africa, and is still an important part of Freedom Day celebrations each year.

Namibia

Red, blue and green, used on the flag of Namibia, are important to the country's native Ovambo people.

1 São Tomé & Príncipe
2 Equatorial Guinea
3 Gabon
4 Congo
5 Democratic Republic of the Congo
6 Uganda
7 Kenya
8 Rwanda
9 Burundi
10 Angola
11 Zambia
12 Tanzania
13 Malawi
14 Namibia
15 Botswana
16 Zimbabwe
17 Mozambique
18 Seychelles
19 Comoros
20 South Africa
21 Swaziland
22 Lesotho
23 Madagascar
24 Mauritius

Southern Africa

includes the huge island of Madagascar, as well as a number of small island groups, such as São Tomé & Príncipe.

Tanzania

Tanganyika and Zanzibar joined together in 1964 to become Tanzania. Their flags were combined to create the Tanzanian flag.

Democratic Republic of the Congo

The flag of this country, which used to be known as Zaïre, was adopted in 2006. The star symbolizes a brilliant future for the country.

WORKING TOGETHER

The Southern African Development Community (SADC) is a group made up of fifteen countries, including Botswana, Tanzania and Mozambique. It works hard to improve life for the people of Southern Africa. The SADC flag shows a green circle (representing animal and plant life) on dark blue (water and sky), with a yellow logo.

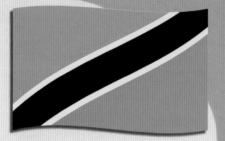

Angola

The emblem in the middle of the Angolan flag features a cog-wheel, a machete and a gold star. It symbolizes the hard-working people of Angola.

Angola celebrated the opening of a new rail line in 2008, connecting the cities of Malanje and Luanda. The trains were painted to match the national flag.

NORTHERN EUROPE

Eight independent nations make up the Nordic Countries (Scandinavia) and Baltic States.

With fiery red volcanoes, bright blue waters and cold, snowy-white winters, the beauty of these nations is reflected in their flags. The Scandinavian countries have often avoided being involved in war, and as a result their flags have remained unchanged for hundreds of years.

SCANDINAVIA

All five Scandinavian countries – Iceland, Norway, Sweden, Finland and Denmark – fly flags that feature a Nordic cross. Also known as a Scandinavian cross, the design symbolizes Christianity. It was first used on the Danish flag, or *Dannebrog*. One of the easiest ways to recognize the design is by the vertical part of the cross. Instead of being in the middle of the flag, it's placed towards the left, or hoist, edge.

Finland

The blue of the Finnish national flag represents the country's many lakes, and the white stands for the snow that covers Finland in winter.

Sweden

The Swedish flag has featured a yellow cross on a blue background for over 500 years.

Denmark

Dannebrog, which means 'Danish cloth', is the flag of Denmark. It's the oldest national flag in the world to still be in use today.

> **Swedish National Day**, or Flag Day, is celebrated each year on June 6. People across the country fly flags and eat *nationaldagsbakelse* – special flag-topped strawberry and marzipan cakes.

The Danish ensign is known as the *Splittflag*. It has a forked or swallow-tail end, and is a darker shade of red than the flag used on land.

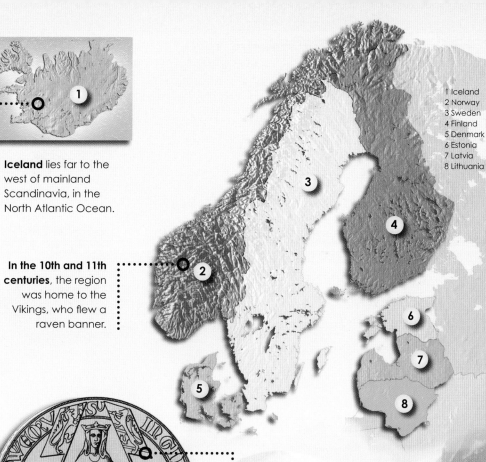

Iceland lies far to the west of mainland Scandinavia, in the North Atlantic Ocean.

1 Iceland
2 Norway
3 Sweden
4 Finland
5 Denmark
6 Estonia
7 Latvia
8 Lithuania

In the 10th and 11th centuries, the region was home to the Vikings, who flew a raven banner.

The seal of the Norwegian Duchess of Ingebjørg from 1318 shows the earliest-known picture of Norway's flag. At that time, it was red with a golden lion in the middle. The design is used today as the royal standard.

Iceland

The flag of Iceland was adopted in 1915, when a red cross was added to the original blue and white design.

Norway

The flag of Norway was based on the *Dannebrog*, and adopted in 1905. Official Norwegian flag days include Christmas Day and the Queen's birthday.

The Danish royal yacht is named *Dannebrog* after the national flag, which it flies as an ensign. It is used by the royal family on cruises and official visits, and can also serve as a hospital-ship.

THE BALTIC STATES

After being ruled by Russia for almost 50 years, all three Baltic states won back their independence in 1991. They also re-adopted their original national flags.

Estonia

The very first blue, black and white Estonian flag is in the national museum.

Lithuania

The red, green and yellow of the flag were often used in folk weavings.

Latvia

The Latvian flag is flown on eleven national flag days each year.

Estonia's flag is raised every day over Pikk Hermann tower in the capital city, Tallinn.

WESTERN EUROPE

The flags of Western Europe mostly have simple designs, often with just three bands.

Countries such as France, Germany and the United Kingdom have been established as independent nations for many centuries. This means their flags have seen fewer changes than those of some younger or more unsettled countries. Designs such as France's *tricolore* have inspired other flags around the world.

EUROPEAN UNION

All the larger countries in Western Europe, except Switzerland, are members of the European Union (EU). A few small countries are non-members. The EU was formed in 1993 to bring countries together and make Europe stronger. The Flag of Europe, which is also the emblem of the EU, shows a circle of 12 gold stars on a blue background.

BELGIUM

The Dukes of Brabant were important Belgian landowners. Belgium combined the black, yellow and red from their coat of arms with the vertical bands of the French *tricolore* to create a bold national flag.

Coat of arms of the Dukes of Brabant

Belgian national flag

France

The national flag of France, the *tricolore*, was adopted in 1794 during the French Revolution.

Bastille Day, on July 14, is a French national holiday. Flags are flown and huge celebrations take place in France and other French-speaking countries.

Luxembourg

Before 1830, Luxembourg didn't have a flag. The current design has been used since the 1840s, but wasn't officially adopted until 1972.

United Kingdom

Three flags make up the Union Jack: St George's Cross (for England), St Andrew's Cross (for Scotland) and St Patrick's Cross (for Ireland).

Every year, Britain's Queen Elizabeth II inspects her Guards. During the grand ceremony, the Guards troop a regimental flag in front of the Queen. Union Jacks line the parade.

GERMANY

The Holy Roman Empire was a group of countries, including Germany, that joined together during the Middle Ages. Its banner showed a black, two-headed eagle with red claws on a gold background. Black, red and gold are still used on the German flag today.

Banner of the Holy Roman Empire

German national flag

Western Europe covers quite a small area of the world, but includes some very rich and powerful countries.

1 Ireland
2 United Kingdom
3 France
4 Andorra
5 Monaco
6 Belgium
7 Luxembourg
8 Netherlands
9 Germany
10 Switzerland
11 Liechtenstein
12 Austria

The Netherlands

The Netherlands' original flag was orange, white and blue. The orange dye often turned red over time, so red was used from the 1700s.

Ireland

Orange represents support for William of Orange. Green stands for Gaelic tradition. White symbolizes peace between the two sides.

SWITZERLAND

Switzerland's national flag is one of only two national flags that are square (the other is the flag of the Vatican City).

Swiss national flag

Austria

The Austrian flag is one of the oldest in the world. Red and white bands have been used as a national emblem for over 800 years, and first appeared on a flag in 1230.

The state flag of Austria is waved proudly by Austrian world-champion ski jumper Thomas Morgenstern. The emblem in the middle of the flag is the national coat of arms.

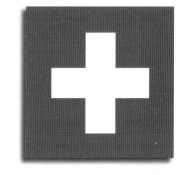

Queen's Day is an exciting national holiday in the Netherlands. Children and adults wear orange and fly the flag to celebrate!

EASTERN EUROPE

History and traditions play an important part in the flags of Eastern Europe.

After World War II, many Eastern European countries had Communist governments. Together, they were known as the Eastern Bloc, and some became part of the Soviet Union. In the early 1990s, many countries gained their independence and changed their flags, or re-adopted old ones, to signal a new stage in their history.

HUNGARIAN HOLE

After World War II, the government in Hungary changed, and Hungarians lost many of their rights. Led by a man named Mátyás Rákosi, the new government added its coat of arms to the national flag. In 1956, the people of Hungary fought against Rákosi's government and won back their flag, as well as their freedom.

From 1949 to 1956, the Hungarian flag displayed Mátyás Rákosi's coat of arms.

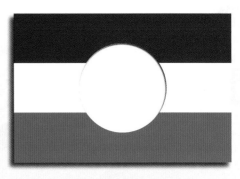

During the 1956 revolution, Hungarians cut out the coat of arms to leave a hole.

Hungary

The red of the modern Hungarian flag stands for strength, the white represents freedom and the green is for hope.

Slovakia

The emblem on the Slovak flag is the country's coat of arms. Without it, the design would be identical to the national flag of Russia.

Poland

The flag of Poland was officially adopted in 1919. The flags of Indonesia and Monaco are very similar, but unrelated – they show a red band over a white one.

Czech Republic

In 1993, Czechoslovakia split into two separate countries, Slovakia and the Czech Republic. The Czechs kept the original Czechoslovakian flag and the Slovaks adopted a new one.

The Polish flag flies over the Polish parliament (shown here) and the presidential palace in Warsaw all the time. Many Polish people display the flag on public holidays and special occasions.

The nations of **Eastern Europe** are sometimes described as the Slavic countries.

The woven pattern on the flag of Belarus symbolizes native plants and flowers. It's also used to decorate traditional costumes and ceremonial serving towels.

1 Poland
2 Belarus
3 Ukraine
4 Czech Republic
5 Slovakia
6 Hungary
7 Romania
8 Moldova

Belarus

When the flag of Belarus is flown at an event or ceremony, the flagpole has to be decorated with a golden, diamond-shaped finial, or topper.

Ukraine

Ukraine first flew its flag in 1918, and it re-adopted it in 1992 after gaining independence from the Soviet Union.

Romania

From 1859 to 1866, the three bands on Romania's flag were horizontal instead of vertical.

Moldova

The emblem on the Moldovan flag only appears on the front. It's one of just a few countries whose flag has two different sides.

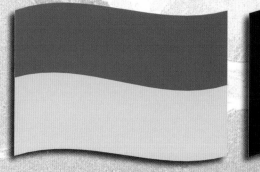

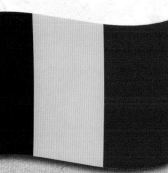

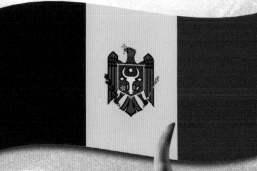

Blue and yellow have been associated with Ukraine for many centuries. On the flag, blue represents the sky and yellow the country's wheat fields.

An aurochs (an extinct type of cow), an eagle, a star, a rose, a cross and an olive branch all feature on the Moldovan coat of arms.

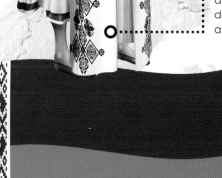

SOUTHERN EUROPE

Almost all of the countries in Southern Europe have coasts that border the Mediterranean Sea.

Many of the countries in this region have long and interesting nautical histories, and this has influenced the designs of their national flags. The red-and-yellow design of the current Spanish flag is based on a naval ensign from the 18th century. In 1978, Greece also adopted a former ensign as its land flag. In the case of Portugal, both the flag and the coat of arms represent the country's important seafaring tradition.

An armillary sphere, like the one on Portugal's national flag, helped sailors and explorers find their way at sea.

Serbia

The Serbian national flag is un upside-down version of the flag of Russia.

Greece

The cross on the national flag of Greece represents the Greek Orthodox religion.

Portugal

The Portuguese flag was adopted in 1911, but the coat of arms in the middle is much older.

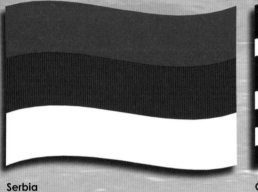

Albania

Albania's flag, with its bold two-headed eagle, is the only black-and-red national flag.

Italy

Italy's flag, also known as *Il Tricolore*, was first used by Napoleon in 1797. After many changes, the design was re-adopted at the end of World War II.

Italians celebrate Republic Day on June 2 each year. Flags fly at a grand military parade in Rome, and planes trail green, white and red smoke!

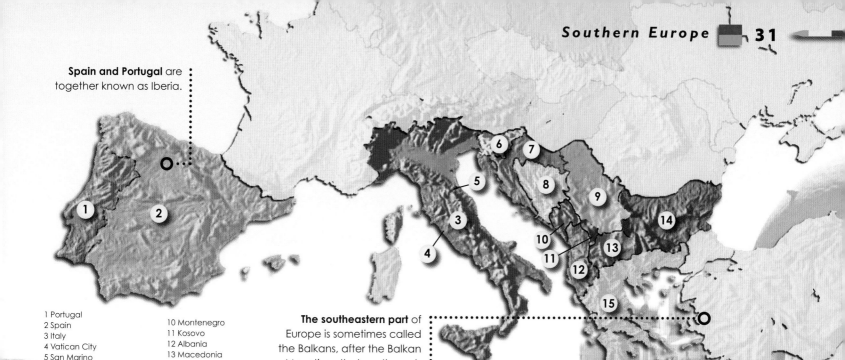

Spain and Portugal are together known as Iberia.

1 Portugal
2 Spain
3 Italy
4 Vatican City
5 San Marino
6 Slovenia
7 Croatia
8 Bosnia and Herzegovina
9 Serbia

10 Montenegro
11 Kosovo
12 Albania
13 Macedonia
14 Bulgaria
15 Greece
16 Malta
17 Cyprus

The southeastern part of Europe is sometimes called the Balkans, after the Balkan Mountians that run through Bulgaria and Serbia.

Bulgaria

In 2007, to celebrate Liberation Day, a bank in the Bulgarian city of Sofia was completely covered – from roof to pavement – in a red, green and white flag!

A huge Spanish flag is hoisted in Plaza de Colón, Madrid. The biggest in Spain, it measures 70ft (21m) by 46ft (14m) and flies from a flagpole that is 165ft (50m) tall.

Bosnia and Herzegovina

The yellow triangle represents the shape of the country.

Spain

The yellow band on the Spanish flag is twice the width of each red band.

Croatia

The red-and-white check pattern on the coat of arms has been a symbol of Croatia for over 1,000 years.

Slovenia

The national flag of Slovenia is very similar to the Slovakian and Russian flags.

Mount Triglav, Slovenia's highest peak, features on the national flag. When Slovenia declared independence from Yugoslavia in 1991, the national flag was flown from the mountain's summit to celebrate the event.

ASIA

As well as Russia, Central Asia and Southern Asia, this region includes the Middle East.

For over 500 years, part of this region (Turkey and the Middle East) was ruled by the Ottoman Empire. Countries including Iraq, Jordan and Kuwait flew the Ottoman flag, which changed almost twenty times before the empire ended in 1922. Another very significant flag change in the region came in 1991, when the Soviet Union collapsed.

REPRESENTING RELIGION

The people of Asia belong to many different religions. Some countries have chosen to represent these on their national flags. An emblem might be a very clear symbol of a religion, such as the Jewish Star of David on Israel's national flag, or something less obvious, such as the green background of the Saudi Arabian flag, which represents Islam. On the flag of Bhutan, yellow stands for secular authority, and orange for the religious authority of Buddhism.

India celebrates Republic Day on January 26. Many of the forty million Indian flags sold each year are waved on this important national holiday.

The Indian flag is a symbol of freedom. Orange stands for self-sacrifice, white for light and purity and green for life and nature. The blue Ashoka wheel represents forward movement and peaceful change.

India

According to the Indian Flag Code, all national flags must be made from *khadi*, a traditional cotton cloth that is spun and woven by hand.

RUSSIA

In 1917, the Russians fought to replace their ruler, the Tsar, with a new government. They eventually formed the Soviet Union and flew the Soviet flag. Then, in 1991, Russia became an independent nation again, and re-adopted its original red, blue and white design.

The flag of the Soviet Union

Russia's national flag

PAN-ARABIC

The red, black, white and green flags of several Middle Eastern countries, including Jordan, Syria and the United Arab Emirates, are described as Pan-Arabic. They were inspired by the flag of the Arab Revolt, which was flown during World War I. It featured three bands (black, green and white) with a red triangle at the hoist edge.

Pakistan

The flag of Pakistan, the 'crescent and star', is so important to the country that it's mentioned in the country's national anthem!

Asia extends from Europe to the Pacific Ocean. More than 60 percent of Russia is in Asia.

1 Turkey
2 Syria
3 Lebanon
4 Israel
5 Jordan
6 Saudi Arabia
7 Yemen
8 Oman
9 United Arab Emirates
10 Qatar
11 Bahrain
12 Kuwait
13 Iraq
14 Iran
15 Russia
16 Georgia
17 Armenia
18 Azerbaijan
19 Turkmenistan
20 Uzbekistan
21 Kazakhstan
22 Kyrgyzstan
23 Tajikistan
24 Afghanistan
25 Pakistan
26 India
27 Nepal
28 Bhutan
29 Bangladesh
30 Maldives
31 Sri Lanka

Kazakhstan

The sun on Kazakhstan's flag represents energy and wealth, and the eagle stands for freedom.

Afghanistan

The flag of Afghanistan has been changed more often than that of any other country in the last 100 years.

Israel

Israel's flag was adopted in 1948. It is based on a traditional blue and white striped Jewish prayer shawl, or *tallit*.

Iraq

Arabic script, like that on Iraq's flag, reads from right to left, so the flag is hoisted on the right-hand side.

Saudi Arabia

Saudia Arabia's flag features the *shahada*, a vow of faith, and is considered holy.

Turkey

The star and crescent moon have been symbols of the Turkish people for hundreds of years.

ASIA

The national flags of eastern Asia are as varied and interesting as the region's peoples.

Many of the flags in this region reflect ancient cultures and traditions, as well as religions, including Buddhism, Hindusim and Taoism. Some are also influenced by the European countries that ruled over almost all of Southeast Asia during the 19th century. Many countries fought to regain their independence, and peace has become a common theme on their flags.

MAKING CHANGES

Adopting a new national flag can take a long time. In 2006, the government of Myanmar decided to change the country's flag. A new one was designed, but a group of judges rejected it. The design was improved, and in 2008 the people of Myanmar voted to adopt it as their national flag from 2010 onwards.

JAPAN

The national flag of Japan is known as Hinomaru. The red circle in the middle represents the rising sun. The Japanese emperor has his own flag, which features a gold chrysanthemum with sixteen petals.

National flag of Japan

The Japanese imperial flag

Vietnam

For many years, North and South Vietnam flew different flags. When the two were united in 1975, the northern flag was adopted by the whole country.

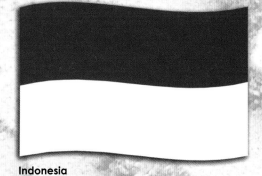

Indonesia

The Indonesian flag was first flown at the country's Independence Day ceremony in 1945. The original flag is kept in a gold-plated case inside the national monument.

Thailand

The red of Thailand's flag stands for the Thai people, white for religion and blue represents royalty. On the naval ensign, a sacred white elephant is also featured.

Cambodia

The national flag of Cambodia is the only national flag to include a building (the temple of Angkor Wat) as part of its design.

Mongolia

The golden Soyombo is a national symbol of Mongolia. On the flag since 1921, it represents freedom and independence.

Malaysia

Malaysia's flag (the Jalur Gemilang, or 'Stripes of Glory') has 14 stripes and a 14-point star, representing 13 states plus the government.

1 Mongolia
2 China
3 North Korea
4 South Korea
5 Japan
6 Myanmar
7 Laos
8 Thailand
9 Cambodia
10 Vietnam
11 Malaysia
12 Singapore
13 Indonesia
14 Brunei
15 Philippines

Many of the countries in this region also fly the Association of Southeast Asian Nations flag, which features an emblem of rice stalks on a blue background.

Singapore

In Singapore, most school classrooms display the national flag. Pupils swear an oath, or National Pledge, to their country in front of the flag each day.

South Korea

The South Korean flag features a red and blue Yin-Yang symbol, which represents balance. The four black trigrams stand for earth, air, fire and water.

China

In 1949, when the People's Republic of China was formed, the Chinese leader Mao Zedong hoisted the current national flag for the first time in the capital city of Beijing.

On the morning of Chinese new year, the national flag is raised and thousands of Chinese people around the world celebrate. Teams of dancers wear huge dragon or lion costumes and parade through the streets to frighten away evil spirits.

AUSTRALIA AND THE PACIFIC ISLANDS

About half of Oceania's national flags feature stars as part of their design.

On the flags of Australia, New Zealand, Samoa and Papua New Guinea, the stars make up the Southern Cross constellation, which can only be seen from the world's southern hemisphere.

AUSTRALIA

The first flag flown in Australia was the Union Jack, displayed when British explorers arrived in 1788. The anniversary of the date is celebrated as Australia Day, a national holiday, but now the flags waved are Australian!

NEW ZEALAND

The national flag of New Zealand features a Union Jack, which symbolizes the country's links with Great Britain. However, some people believe the flag should be changed to reflect New Zealand's Maori history and traditions, too.

PAPUA NEW GUINEA

Papua New Guinea's flag was adopted in 1971. It was designed by a 15-year-old schoolgirl, and was the winning entry in a national competition.

The national flag of Papua New Guinea

Raggiana bird of paradise

The raggiana bird of paradise is Papua New Guinea's national bird.

Sydney Harbour Bridge, one of Australia's most famous landmarks, often flies flags to mark special occasions and events.

NEW ZEALAND

As well as the national flag, New Zealand has a popular unofficial flag. The Silver Fern is a state emblem, and also features on the coat of arms and New Zealand's one-dollar coin.

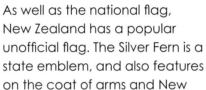

The Silver Fern, the unofficial flag of New Zealand

The national flag of New Zealand

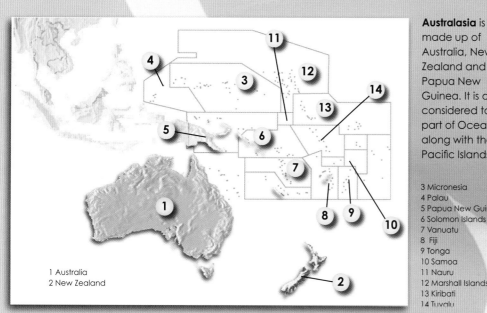

1 Australia
2 New Zealand

Australasia is made up of Australia, New Zealand and Papua New Guinea. It is also considered to be part of Oceania, along with the Pacific Islands.

3 Micronesia
4 Palau
5 Papua New Guinea
6 Solomon Islands
7 Vanuatu
8 Fiji
9 Tonga
10 Samoa
11 Nauru
12 Marshall Islands
13 Kiribati
14 Tuvalu

THE PACIFIC ISLANDS

Altogether, there are over 20,000 islands in the Pacific Ocean. People inhabit about half of them. Water is an important part of island life, both for catching fish to eat and keeping their land healthy, so many of Oceania's flags represent water in some way.

The flags of Australia and New Zealand are both based on the British state ensign.

Australia

One of Australia's biggest flags can be seen above Parliament House in Canberra. It's 42ft (12.8m) wide by 21ft (6.4m) high and flies from a flagpole 265ft (81m) tall.

PACIFIC ISLANDS

The Pacific Islands are usually divided into three groups: Polynesia, Melanesia, and Micronesia.

Nauru

The flag of Nauru shows the island's position in the world just below the Equator (the yellow line).

Solomon Islands

The stars stand for five island-groups, the blue is the sea, yellow the sunshine and green the land.

Tonga

Tonga's original flag (1875) was identical to the Red Cross flag. It was changed to avoid confusion.

Fiji

On Fiji's flag, bright blue represents the Pacific Ocean, which is important to the life of the islanders.

Vanuatu

On the yellow emblem, the boar's tusk symbolizes wealth and success and the fern represents peace.

INTERNATIONAL FLAGS

Some groups and organizations have flags that are recognized all over the world.

In 1988, a World Flag was designed as a global symbol of togetherness and strength. Most international flags have a similar purpose and represent people or nations joining together to achieve something positive. In situations where members all speak different languages and come from different cultures, a flag is easy to recognize and can quickly unite people who share a goal.

THE EUROPEAN UNION

The European Union, or EU, is made up of 27 countries in Europe. They work together to make life easier and better for 500 million European people, and also donate money to help countries in poorer parts of the world. Together with 23 official languages, a motto and a European anthem, the EU also has its own blue and gold flag. Many countries fly the EU flag alongside their national flag outside government buildings, and it is also used as an emblem on European driving licenses and Euro coins.

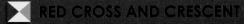

RED CROSS AND CRESCENT

The International Red Cross and Red Crescent Movement protects people who are ill or suffering around the world. It's especially important in places at war or suffering a natural disaster. Workers are easily recognized by the red cross or crescent symbol they display on clothes and vehicles.

The Red Crescent flag

The Red Cross flag

The 50th anniversary of the Treaty of Rome, which sets out the basis of the EU, was celebrated in Berlin in 2007. The city held a huge street party and released balloons in the same shade of blue as the EU flag.

The flag of the European Union has a blue background representing the Western world, and 12 gold stars standing for completeness and perfection. The circle represents unity.

NATO MEMBER COUNTRIES

Founder members 1949	Joined 1952	Joined 2004
Canada	Greece	Bulgaria
United States	Turkey	Estonia
Iceland		Latvia
Norway	**Joined 1955**	Lithuania
Denmark	Germany (as	Romania
United Kingdom	West Germany)	Slovakia
France (fully		Slovenia
re-joined 2009)	**Joined 1982**	
Belgium	Spain	**Joined 2009**
Luxembourg		Albania
The Netherlands	**Joined 1999**	Croatia
Italy	Czech Republic	
Portugal	Poland	
	Hungary	

The countries in red are all members of NATO. When it was formed in 1949, NATO had 12 members. Since then, another 16 nations have joined and more are likely to be invited in the future.

NATO

NATO (the North Atlantic Treaty Organization) joins together 28 countries in Europe and America that help to protect and keep each other safe. It also works with other countries to solve problems in a peaceful way. Countries that are members can fly the NATO flag alongside their national flags and ensigns.

The official emblem of NATO, which features on its flag, is a compass rose – a map symbol that points north, south, east and west.

The flag of the United Nations features a map of the world surrounded by olive branches, an international symbol of peace.

THE WORLD SCOUT FLAG

The fleur-de-lis, often used as a symbol for north on maps, symbolizes showing the way in doing one's duty and helping others. The rope links Scouts from around the world.

The World Scout Flag

UNITED NATIONS

The United Nations was set up after World War II in the hope of preventing more wars and achieving world peace. It also aims to improve life for people in difficult situations around the globe. All 192 UN member-countries are considered equal, and to show this their flags are flown in alphabetical order.

UN peacekeepers arrive soon after a war has ended. Their flags and blue hats or helmets help to identify them.

SIGNAL FLAGS

In 1857, a code was created so ships could exchange important messages.

The International Code of Signals means more than 70,000 different signals can be communicated using flags, flashing lights or Morse code. It acts as an international language, with ships from anywhere in the world able to display and read messages.

MARITIME SIGNAL FLAGS

The flags used by the code each have a particular meaning, as well as relating to a letter of the alphabet. They can be used on their own or in groups to spell out words or communicate special set messages. These might be distress signals, important weather warnings or other kinds of urgent information for other ships.

A (Alpha)
Diver down, keep clear

B (Bravo)
Dangerous cargo

C (Charlie)
Yes

D (Delta)
Keep clear

E (Echo)
Altering course to starboard

F (Foxtrot)
Disabled

G (Golf)
Want a pilot

H (Hotel)
Pilot on board

I (India)
Altering course to port

J (Juliet)
On fire, keep clear

K (Kilo)
Desire to communicate

L (Lima)
Stop instantly

M (Mike)
I am stopped

N (November)
No

O (Oscar)
Man overboard

P (Papa)
About to sail

Q (Quebec)
Request pratique (license or permission to use a port)

R (Romeo)

S (Sierra)
Engines 'going astern'

T (Tango)
Keep clear

U (Uniform)
You are running into danger

V (Victor)
Require assistance

W (Whiskey)
Require medical assistance

X (Xray)
Stop your intention

Y (Yankee)
Am dragging anchor

Z (Zulu)
Require a tug

SEMAPHORE

Semaphore is a way of sending messages using two hand-held flags. The flags are usually red and yellow squares, divided in half diagonally. To signal alphabet letters, numbers or short set messages, they are held in a series of different patterns and positions. At night, lighted sticks or wands are used instead of flags.

Flag positions used in semaphore

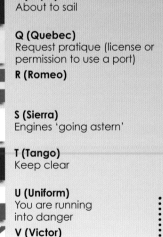

A dressed ship is either at anchor or on its first or last voyage of the day.

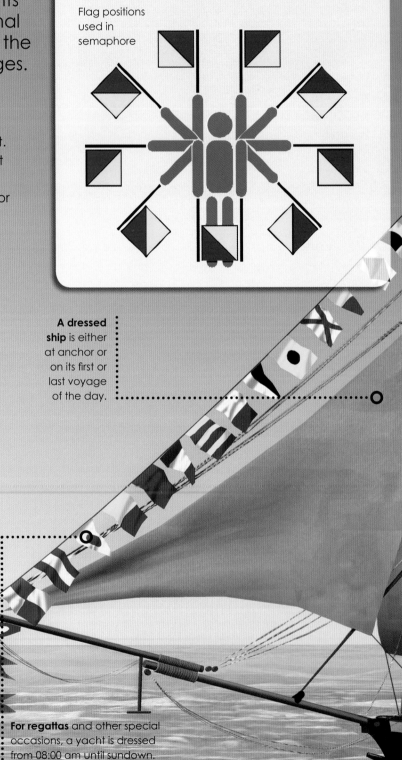

For regattas and other special occasions, a yacht is dressed from 08:00 am until sundown.

DRESSING OVERALL

Decorating a ship with flags is known as dressing, or dressing overall. The signal flags and pennants are strung on a line, called a dressing line, from the bow (front) to the stern (back). A national flag can also be flown from the masthead. Dressing is usually done on special or ceremonial occasions, such as a country's national or flag day.

ANSWER PENNANT

An answer pennant is used to let another ship know its message has been seen and understood. The flag is set halfway when the ship starts to receive the signal, then hoisted right up once the message ends.

The substitute, or repeater, flags stand in for any letter. They allow messages that use a character more than once to be sent more easily.

Twenty-six rectangular alphabet flags, plus three substitute pennants, feature clear, bold combinations of red, blue, black, white and yellow.

NUMBER FLAGS

In addition to the alphabet flags, there are ten numeric pennants, used to communicate numbers. NATO navies also use another ten number flags. The answer pennant is used to represent a decimal point.

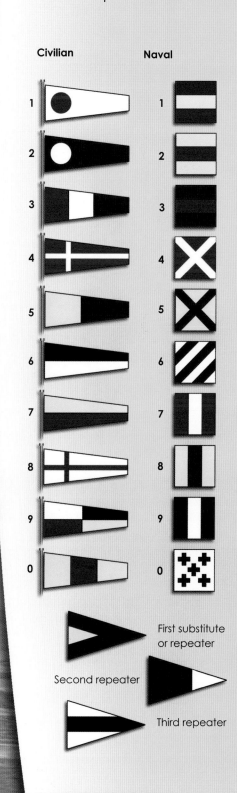

Civilian / Naval

1 2 3 4 5 6 7 8 9 0

First substitute or repeater

Second repeater

Third repeater

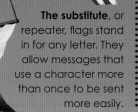

Sports and Safety Flags

Flags are used in many sports as a quick way of communicating information.

From golf courses and racetracks to beaches and ski-slopes, flags are easily, and often internationally, recognized symbols. But unlike most other kinds of flag, they can also save lives. By learning to recognize just a few different flags, people can enjoy their hobbies and stay safe at the same time.

At the finish line, a black-and-white chequered flag is waved to signal the end of the race. The first driver to 'take', or pass, the flag is usually the winner.

FLAGS IN MOTOR RACING

Flags are used in motor racing to pass on important messages and warnings to drivers. They're usually waved by a marshal, or flagman, near the start and finish line, or at particular points around the racetrack. It's important that they're clearly seen and understood by drivers at high speed, so the flags are bright and bold. A flag is lowered to start most motor-racing events, and also to signal the end of a race. Similar flags are used in motorcycle racing and go-karting.

Unsporting warning flag

Driver must call in at the pit

Let the faster driver overtake

Oil on the track

Mechanical problem warning flag

Race must stop

In Formula One motor racing, the national flag is used to start a race. A yellow flag signals danger, and white indicates a slow-moving vehicle on the track.

DIVING FLAGS

Diving flags are usually flown from boats to signal that divers are under the surface of the water. Other boats know to keep a safe distance away (100–200yds/ 91–182m). Divers themselves must stay within 50yds (45m) of the flag.

The Diver Down flag means do not approach. It is required by law in the US, Canada, Italy and some other countries.

The Alpha flag is internationally recognized and commonly used in Europe. It shows that a boat has divers or equipment beneath the water.

The Papa flag signals a dive is over. It warns that divers may be surfacing and the boat is about to sail.

Scuba divers sometimes display their Diver Down flag on a floating surface-marker buoy instead of a boat.

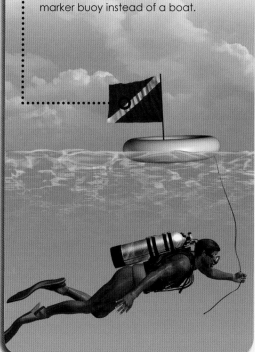

Danger

Surfing and watercraft

Lifeguard on patrol

Do not use inflatables

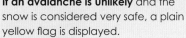

If an avalanche is unlikely and the snow is considered very safe, a plain yellow flag is displayed.

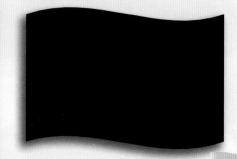

If avalanches are likely, a black flag is flown to signal danger. Black-flag areas should always be avoided.

Lifeguards on duty patrol between the red-and-yellow flags, making this the safest area for swimmers.

Beach safety flags are used and recognized around the world. They let beachgoers know when and where it's safe to swim, surf, dive and use inflatables in the water.

Avalanches kill more and more people every year. Experts work out where an avalanche might happen, and put up warning flags. Yellow-and- black checks mean there's a high-to-medium risk.

FASCINATING FACTS

All flags are special to the country that flies them, but some really stand out from the crowd.

The flag of Nepal is the only national flag that isn't a rectangle, while Libya is unique in flying a plain flag with no pattern, symbols or emblems. The flags of some countries have made it into the record books for being especially tall, small, old or unusual in some other way.

SMALLEST FLAG

The world's smallest representation of a flag is so tiny that it is invisible to the human eye! It's etched onto a silicon chip, and is more than ten times smaller in height than the width of a single hair, but still includes all 50 stars and 13 stripes of the US national flag.

The world's biggest national flag was unfurled in Israel in 2007. The record-breaking blue-and-white Israeli flag covered an area of 18,843 sq m (202,824 sq ft). It was laid out on the ground, as it was far too big to fly from a flagpole!

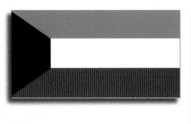

The world's biggest kite to be decorated as a flag carried the design of Kuwait's national flag. Made in 2004, it was shaped like a giant pillowcase and took 750 hours to make.

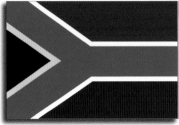

The only national flag to include six different shades but no emblem is South Africa's national flag, which is officially described as being 'black, gold, green, white, chilli-red and blue.'

The tallest unsupported flagpole in the world is in Turkmenistan. Standing at 133m (436ft) tall, it flies a huge Turkmenistan national flag that is about as big as two tennis courts!

The world's tallest supported flagpole is in North Korea, in the village of Gijeong-dong. The160m (525ft) tall tower flies North Korea's national flag.

The world's biggest regularly hoisted flag – measuring 70 x 100m (230 x 330ft) and weighing 600kg (1,300lbs) when dry – is the national flag that flies over Brazil's capital city, Brasilia.

The oldest-known national flag still in use is the Danish *Dannebrog*. It dates back to the 14th century, and inspired other Scandinavian countries to use a similar cross design on their flags.

Netherlands

Russia   India

The oldest *tricolore* still flying today is the flag of The Netherlands. When it originally appeared in 1572, it was orange, white and blue, but the orange was later replaced with red, which is a more stable dye. Many other countries now fly *tricolores*, including Russia and India.

The most commonly used flag is the British Union Jack. Many countries that were once British colonies include it on their flags.

INSPIRATIONAL FLAGS

Once you start noticing flags, it's easy to see that many have similar or common designs, from stripes and bands to crosses, stars and emblems. This isn't a coincidence! For as long as national flags have been around, countries have been influenced and inspired by the designs they see being flown by other nations. Sometimes this happens with countries that are close to each other and have similar histories, but a country may also admire something about a nation much further away and take inspiration from their flag and what it symbolizes.

Costa Rica

Dominican Republic

Haiti

Italy

One of the most inspirational flags is the French *Tricolore*. This symbol of revolution has influenced the flags of Costa Rica, the Dominican Republic, Haiti and, in design, Italy.

Uruguay

Liberia

Chile

Malaysia

Representing revolution and freedom, the American 'Stars and Stripes' has influenced countries such as Uruguay, Liberia, Chile and Malaysia.

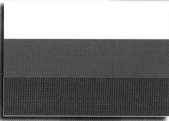

Slovenia

Slovakia

Serbia

Croatia

Pan-Slavic red, white and blue, as on Russia's national flag, have been adopted by many Eastern European countries.

Senegal

Togo

Ghana

Mali

Pan-African green, gold and red, first used on the Ethiopian flag, are used by Senegal, Togo, Ghana and Mali, among many others.

Algeria

Azerbaijan

Comoros

Malaysia

The crescent design on Turkey's flag represents Islam. Many Muslim countries have been inspired by it, including Algeria, Azerbaijan, the Comoros and Malaysia.

Iraq

Jordan

Kuwait

Syria

Red, white, black and green – the Pan-Arab shades – are taken from the flag of the Arab Revolt, which was flown during World War I. Today, they're used on eleven national flags in the region (though not all of them use green). Examples include the flags of Iraq, Jordan, Kuwait and Syria.

Colombia

Ecuador

Venezuela's national flag, which symbolized the fight for independence when it was first adopted, inspired the flags of Colombia and Ecuador.

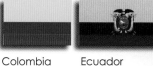

Vietnam

Angola

The red and gold Soviet flag, with its hammer and sickle design, inspired the national flags of other Communist countries, such as Vietnam and Angola, as well as many national Communist Party flags.

GLOSSARY

Arab Revolt (1916–18) A fight by Arab countries to win their independence from the Ottoman Empire and set up a single Arab state.

Aztec Civilization Group of people with a rich culture who lived in Mexico and Central America from the 14th–16th century.

Bastille Day A French national holiday commemorating the storming of the Bastille prison in Paris, which started the French Revolution.

Colonies, Thirteen The thirteen original United States of America, known as British America before the War of Independence.

Communist A person who believes that a country's government should control the economy, and that the wealth should be shared equally.

Crusades A series of military expeditions in the 11th, 12th and 13th centuries by European Christians. They fought to reclaim the Holy Land (Middle East) from Muslim rule.

Daimyo Powerful land-owners who ruled with military force over most of Japan from the 10th–19th century.

Ensign Version of a national flag flown on ships or military vessels.

French Revolution (1789–99) Period of change and violence in France, when poor people fought to win equal rights with the rich.

Frontiersman An early US settler who lived on the border between developed and wild land.

Heraldry The 900-year-old study of designing or interpreting coats of arms, and the history of the families they represent.

Inca Civilization A sophisticated empire in western South America (13th–16th century).

Knights Templars A group of Christian monks who fought in the Crusades.

Mon Symbols or crests, the Japanese equivalent of a coat of arms.

Morse Code Code sent by radio, with letters and numbers represented by strings of short and long signals (written as dots and dashes).

New World A phrase used by Europeans to describe lands they discovered – first the Americas, and then Australasia.

Ottoman Empire Military rule based in Turkey from 1299 to 1923, governing countries in southern Europe, Asia and North Africa.

Pharaohs The rulers of ancient Egypt from roughly 3100 BC to 30 BC.

Pioneer life Way of living adopted by American settlers who moved to undeveloped parts of the country.

Port The left-hand side of a forward-facing boat or ship.

Queen's Day A national holiday marking the official birthday (April 30) of the Queen of the Netherlands.

Ratio In relation to flags, the width and height measurements of a flag.

Saladin Great Muslim leader who recaptured Jerusalem during the Crusades.

Samurai warriors Upper-class Japanese sword-fighters.

Slavic People and language from the eastern part of Europe, dating back to the 6th century.

Starboard The right-hand side of a forward-facing boat or ship.

State ensign A flag flown by official, non-military craft, such as coastguard ships.

Symbol A shape, picture or sign used to represent something else.

Taoism An ancient Chinese religion or belief that encourages a simple, calm and natural way of life.

Trigram A Chinese symbol representing a natural element, such as air, fire or water.

Vatican City The world's smallest country, a walled city within Rome, Italy. Home to the Pope.

Vikings Scandinavian explorers and warriors, who raided and settled in parts of Europe (8th–11th century).

VIP Very Important Person

War of Independence (1775–83) Conflict between Great Britain and the thirteen colonies of North America, which wanted the right to rule themselves.

Washington, George The first US president (in office 1789–97).

William of Orange King William III, born Prince of Orange. He ruled England and Ireland from 1672–1702.

INDEX